I'LL BE
SEEIN' YA

I'LL BE SEEIN' YA:

A PLAY

WITH *THE INSOLVENCIES*

JON ROBIN BAITZ

FARRAR, STRAUS AND GIROUX

NEW YORK

Farrar, Straus and Giroux
120 Broadway, New York 10271

Library of Congress Cataloging-in-Publication Data
Names: Baitz, Jon Robin, 1961– author. | Baitz, Jon Robin,
    1961– Insolvencies.
Title: I'll be seein' ya : a play : with The insolvencies /
    Jon Robin Baitz.
Other titles: I will be seeing you
Description: First edition. | New York : Farrar, Straus and
    Giroux, 2023.
Identifiers: LCCN 2022041854 | ISBN 9780374607715 (paperback)
Subjects: LCGFT: Drama.
Classification: LCC PS3552.A393 I45 2023 | DDC 812/.54—
    dc23/eng/20220909
LC record available at https://lccn.loc.gov/2022041854

www.fsgbooks.com
www.twitter.com/fsgbooks • www.facebook.com/fsgbooks

1 3 5 7 9 10 8 6 4 2

For
Bryan Lourd,
a dear and very wise friend

contents

I'LL BE
SEEIN' YA

Characters

ALICE MURCHOW—in her seventies

MR. SPENCER STILL—an Asian man in his twenties

DORSA YERUSHALAIM—Iranian, in her seventies

JAPHY MURCHOW—Alice's brother, of indeterminate age

Place

The agitated and unsettled Los Angeles of summer 2020.

The city burning is Los Angeles's
deepest image of itself.
—JOAN DIDION

Note

Given that theater was essentially shut down because of the worldwide pandemic, many of us who work in it, instead of postponing productions entirely, made filmed versions of new plays for theaters to stream. We rehearsed this play on the stage of the Kirk Douglas Theatre in October 2021 for three weeks and filmed it there with three cameras during a week in November.

It was directed by Robert Egan, and the cast was Christine Lahti as Allie, Justin Kirk as Japhy, Sussan Deyhim as Dorsa, and Christopher Larkin as Mr. Still.

My brother, the protean composer Rick Baitz, wrote the exquisite score, another happy collaboration between us.

For me, it reaffirmed all the qualities I love in making theater—the process of lifting music out of silence, the odd tension between performance and reality, the magic created by lighting and sound. And it incorporated the control afforded by filming, a strange and very specific hybrid made possible by a hallucinatory and unrelenting virus that forced theater artists to find new ways of putting on shows in barns, as it were.

[SCENE I]

"All the Old Familiar Places"

Summer 2020

*An open-plan apartment off Pico and Robertson Boulevards
in Los Angeles, in what is known in architectural
vernacular as the "dingbat style." The neighborhood is a
polyglot middle-class mix of immigrants and races. Realtors
optimistically list flats here as "Beverly Hills adjacent."
Old Jewish and Persian residents, Somali restaurants, low,
horizontal buildings, young people sharing apartments, and
the retired on fixed incomes.*

*ALLIE MURCHOW, of the last category, is pulling on
makeup in front of a vanity mirror. The hair is blond.
"I'll Be Seeing You" plays very softly from a telephone's
speakerphone, an instrumental "hold music" version,
soporific and anodyne.*

Someone knocks on the front door . . .

WOMAN'S VOICE
(Middle Eastern accent)
Allie, darling? Are you there? Allie— It's Dorsa! Please,

if you are there? I'm going to try and make it to the market. You want some lamb shanks or some bananas? Or they may have that super-soft toilet paper?

ALLIE

I'm fine, Dorsa. Thanks, honey. I'm good.

DORSA

. . . Well—you can text me if you change your mind. I think they have organic lamb shanks—good for the skin?

ALLIE

I'm okay for organic lamb shanks and that super-soft toilet paper, sweetie. Also good for the skin . . .

DORSA

Okay . . . wish me luck.

ALLIE

(calm, to herself, as she works on her eyes)

Good luck. The eyes are the hardest part, always. And. *Huh*. Smoky eyes? Please. *Now*? That's in *again*? But I was doing it when we worked at Robinson's department store at the Beverly Hilton in the salon; *I* did it back in '73. And that was—I mean, I did Goldie Hawn, I did Dyan Cannon. Remember? Eydie Gorme and—what's her name? From that show—*Bewitched*—

Elizabeth Montgomery! Smoky eye. Hah. Please, everything from my time. It's all in again, like they just discovered it.

MR. STILL (ON SPEAKER PHONE)
Your call is very important to us here at Nick Stein Pharmacy. Please stay on the line for a pharmacy specialist.

ALLIE
(laughing)
I've been on the line for half an hour. Jesus, what's a girl gotta do to get a *refill* and some Yves Saint Laurent Touche Éclat All-Over Brightening Concealer Pens?

MR. STILL (ON SPEAKER)
Remember, in this time of COVID-19 we are taking extra precautions, so please be prepared by wearing a mask if coming in.

ALLIE
Oh, I'm *"prepared."* I have two masks, and these gloves, and these wipes with one hundred percent alcohol—

MR. STILL (ON SPEAKER)
(over her, cuts her off)
In addition to our pharmacy, we carry a full range of beauty and apothecary products.

ALLIE

Ohhhhh, those English Altoid mints and blackberry throat pastilles. I hope they are on sale . . .

MR. STILL (ON SPEAKER)

All of our specialists are helping other customers. Because of COVID-19, we are busier than usual and hold times may be longer. Please be patient.

ALLIE

I am soooo patient. See! The lash line, the crease where the lid folds into the shape of the eye.

That's where you blend with care and patience. But you must have the right concealer because dark shadows will ruin the look, and boy, do you have dark shadows.

ALLIE *sings along to hold music.*

ALLIE

". . . In everything that's light and gay
I'll always think of you that way . . ."

OUTSIDE, *sound of SIRENS.*

ALLIE

(distracted, irritated)

What's the rest of it? What is the goddamn *rest* of it?

Our staff is busy because of increased call volume due to the COVID-19 epidemic, so please press pound and wait for the beep, and leave a detailed message for the pharmacy. Someone will call you back. Due to the recent spike in COVID cases, we are not doing delivery right now. Thank you.

LOUD BEEP. ALLIE *hits pound.*

ALLIE
(formal and regal)
Hello, this is Allie Murchow. I should be in the system. I am trying to get ahold of three sticks of the YSL Touche Éclat Brightening Pen, and nobody has it. Nobody has them, I mean. I tried, listen, I tried. In Luminous Praline. Or Luminous Sand. I *also* am trying to get a refill of my Respericore. Two milligrams. Ninety pills. ————And . . .
(beat)
(I have the special coupons from the manufacturer for not tolerating the generic. So it can't be full price; it should be in the records. The generic does not agree with me. In fact, I started to have *severe* side effects from the generic. A rash. And then other things—happen. It has to be the *actual* Respericore Plus. Not the generic.)
(beat)
My doctor, Hy Wexler, sent them a letter, and it explained

that I was allergic to— You know some of these generic companies, they change the formula? *They change it. Hah.*

And it can throw you completely out of whack. I was in Du-par's at the Farmer's Market because they have double-dip French toast, and I was being stood up by Cody Garson, who was at the goddamn Du-par's in the Valley, if you can imagine. Cody, who was in the 20th Century Fox Stars of Tomorrow talent program with me in 1969. He went on to Vegas to choreograph at The Sands. But I exploded on the phone when he called my Du-par's. "Tell me, Cody. Why were you so adamant about you and I being in *Planet of the Apes* together? Of course, because no one could see our faces. And then you go to the wrong Du-par's!? Who do you think you're kidding?"

JAPHY MURCHOW *enters in pajama bottoms, barefoot.*
He goes into the kitchen and takes out a water bottle, some snacks.

JAPHY

You leavin' one of your loooooooong Cody messages? To whom, this time? We've talked about this, kiddo.

ALLIE
(shushes him)
Japhy, you know the whole ugly episode, so knock it off!

(to phone)

As I was saying, Cody went to the Du-par's in Studio City, and when he called my Du-par's— Well, there was a rather big scene. A meltdown of sorts. I ended up hospitalized at Cedars-Sinai. It was all because of Cody. And those generic medications. Set me off. So please have someone call me back because I have run out of my good medications.

JAPHY

(an energized idea)

Sis, I'm in the mood for those cold sesame noodles. How about it?

ALLIE

(gestures—shut up)

And *now* you don't deliver! Because of the—the disturbances?? And I am *just* south of Pico and Robertson, which is very close. I don't want to go out right now. With this terrible virus.

JAPHY *sits near her with his snacks and water.*

JAPHY

. . . And the unrest—

ALLIE

And the *unrest.* The problems. The breaking windows. The— I don't, of course, blame any of the people doing it. But. There was a shiva for Lenore Katz from book club. Now there can't be a real shiva. They tried it on the Zoom, but it—it just—*fizzled*. I saw the protestors outside. I saw them. No masks. And—and—look. Let's face it. To this neighborhood? My neighborhood! We didn't do anything— We—

A LOUD BEEP.

MR. STILL (ON SPEAKER)
If you are satisfied with your message, please press pound to deliver. If you would like to rerecord it, please press one and then pound and wait for the beep.

JAPHY
(*patiently*)
Come on, Allie. Rerecord. And get to the point! Meds!

She presses 1 and pound. BEEP.

ALLIE
(*exercising control*)
Hello, this is Allie Murchow. I should be in the system. I am trying to get ahold of three sticks of the YSL Touche Éclat Brightening Pens and nobody has it. Nobody has them, I mean. I tried . . . listen, *I tried*. In Luminous Praline. Or Luminous Sand. And a refill of my prescription.

(trying to remember)

Respiriloc Plus. Two milligrams times 90 or 180 or—I have a special coupon.

More SIRENS. ALLIE *frozen.*

JAPHY

Jesus, Allie? Wow. Ooph. What a moron. Get it straight. Is it Respiriloc or Respiricore Plus?

ALLIE

You know, *you're* my pharmacy. I'm Allie *Murchow*. My family has been using this pharmacy for . . . I mean, Nick used to joke around with me, my only pharmacist since I'm fourteen—and my late parents and my brother . . .

JAPHY

Preach, Reverend Allie!!

ALLIE

I'm—it's really not right *not to pick up.* The YSL Touche Éclat is a concealer and a foundation. It is vital—

JAPHY

Totally vital!

ALLIE

You need it for smoky eyes, which I practically invented when I did Dyan Cannon at Robinson's department store at the Beverly Hilton around the time of the movie *Shampoo*, which I was background in because Dyan was friends with Hal Ashby . . .

JAPHY
(egging her on)
And you told Mom and Dad . . .

ALLIE
Yes, I told my parents, and they were so *proud* that I was an actor, even though it was background, which you can see one hour six minutes or so into the movie, when Warren is cutting someone's hair. Not really, though. And I got Cody in it too. He's one of the waiters at the benefit at the Bistro.

JAPHY
(compassionate)
Then Cody went off to Vegas! To help choreograph . . . Shirley MacLaine's show with all the cute chorus boys . . .

ALLIE
And girls. I mean, yeah, after the whole Du-par's incident, which he caused by going to the wrong Du-par's. Who goes to the Du-par's in the Valley? I realized I needed to move on even if it meant breaking Cody's heart.

JAPHY

Tell him about the El Cholo dinner.

ALLIE

My dad worked at MGM in the cutting room. A cutter. He ran the whole damn thing. And *my mom*—she was in the costume shop at Paramount—and my dad, *that night*, after I shot, after I shot out of *Shampoo*, and my mom, we danced!!! They took us for Mexican at the *old* El Cholo, and we sang, and the three of us danced because they had this Mexican trio and they did "I'll Be Seein' Ya" in Spanish at *our* table! It was a glorious evening of celebration—

JAPHY

At the end of which, dear ole Dad says, "Allie, don't get your hopes up too high. You'll always be a cutter. Just like me. Behind the scenes, *but* . . . never in them." Did I get that right, sis?

(sings in Spanish)

"Te estaré viendo
en todos los viejos lugares conocidos,
que este corazón mío abraza
durante todo el día."

ALLIE *hums song. There is a BEEP.*

MR. STILL (ON SPEAKER)

If you are satisfied with your message, please press pound to deliver. If you would like to rerecord, please press one and pound and wait for the beep.

JAPHY

I think you need some sleep, sis. I mean a good sleep. What pill will make you sleep? Or better yet, what pill will wake you the fuck up? This could be your moment. It's all coming together. Lots of decisions to make!!

She presses 1 and #. BEEP.

ALLIE

Hello, this is Allie Murchow. I should be in the system. I am trying to get ahold of three sticks of the YSL Touche Éclat Brightening Pen. And. I need . . . I need . . . please call me back . . . Okay? I need a refill of . . . of . . . I'm just going to listen to your music for a while alone.

JAPHY exits. ALLIE peers out the window. Sirens. The red light of the police flashers floods the apartment. ALLIE is frozen.

[SCENE II]

"I'll Find You in the Morning Sun"

Later, same day. Sun shafts angle light into the apartment.
Distant chanting, impossible to quite hear, rumbles like a
storm.

Front door suddenly opens. DORSA *is with* ALLIE,
who is the worse for wear, in very large sunglasses, gloves,
mask, baseball cap, and raincoat. She wears a vintage
Emanuel Ungaro dress, right out of Gena Rowlands in
Gloria.

ALLIE

Thank *God* you have the key. Never leave without your
key!!!

DORSA

What happened, Allie? Are you okay?

ALLIE
(agitated)

No, no. I ran into the rioters. They were right outside
Shanghai Winter Palace on Pico, they were right *there*.

DORSA

Calm down, darling. Really, it is not a riot—

ALLIE

Okay, "protests"! You don't understand! I was trying to get shrimp toast and sizzling rice soup and moo shu pork and those sesame noodles—for Japhy—

JAPHY *hovers in the back hall.*

DORSA

Japhy? What do you mean?

ALLIE
(over her)
And some fat girl, a *white* kid, tattoos and *no makeup* or anything—scary, so scary, zeroes in on me, and she screams, "Join us, join us," you know? And I say, "I wish I could, honey. I love you, I love what you're doing and your *look* and the cause and—but I just have to get some Oriental food back home because—" But—but—she just started screaming in my face. "You're the fucking problem—your privilege—your privilege—you exude it . . ." And then she punches me.

Screaming, "*Oriental*, Oriental, *Oriental food*!? Who do you think you are???" She is spitting all over me and—and yells, "Fuck you and your 'Oriental' food! People are dying in the *streets*! Black people are being

shot and strangled and burnt and rocket launchered—
and you want *dim sum*?"

DORSA

Allie, SLOW DOWN!

ALLIE

I don't understand what is *happening* to Los Angeles!
This is West LA. Why here? Who are we? Are we the
cause of— No! No! Look at us. You're an immigrant, for
God's sake, I'm on a fixed income, and that tattooed fat
girl was white.

DORSA

Listen, my dear. You must lie down. Please, deep breaths.
Breathe.

ALLIE

Dorsa, I never thought that in Beverly Hills . . . Is this
what it was like when you left Iran?

DORSA

I never thought it would happen in Tehran! Never!
Until it did. Our chic little hotel with our chic Parisian
cuisine. So cultured, so *harmless*.

Our trendy Courrèges boutique, with the black-
and-white line of miniskirts and pantsuits. That was
a crime to the mullahs. "Western corruption of Islamic

values!" But worse, I taught one of our chefs how to bake a perfect pain au chocolat, proof of me being a Zionist agent.

ALLIE

I am not a Zionist, and I can't bake . . .

DORSA

Allie, be ready. We got out, Rostam and I. Just in time. But you saw how sad Rostam was here. He could not let go of his past! Never ready for the "new realities."

ALLIE

Not everyone is as strong as you. I worry I am like Rostam. Can you—

DORSA

You have to be strong and ready to fight! The mullah madness is here now, lunatic QAnon lizard people in Washington, Nazis running over women in Charlottesville. *Thank God* those protestors are marching, and so should you! Got it? We have entered the "aftertimes."

ALLIE

Aftertimes? Got it! . . . I think.

Sound of demonstrators.

DORSA

Listen. You see? You see? That's my sound. What are we doing *here*? Come on!

ALLIE

No. I'm okay. Right here.

DORSA

Well, I'm going to join them. I'll bring you some tea in a little bit.

ALLIE

Mint. Okay?

DORSA

Okay. Mint.

DORSA *leaves.* JAPHY *comes into the room, jeans and T-shirt, barefoot.*

JAPHY

S'up now?

ALLIE

I got pushed to the ground by a fat girl. She didn't even have a mask, and she breathed all over me, and now what? I have to get some sort of—

JAPHY

Test! I know what that's like. You wait and wait, and if you see a brown spot, you're a goner. I waited in those testing rooms—*alone!* Now it's your turn. If you lose your sense of smell, that's when you know.

ALLIE *looks at* JAPHY, *horrified.*

ALLIE

I can't get sick . . . I stood there knocking at the front door of Shanghai Winter—

JAPHY

For egg roll, sizzling rice soup, and my sesame noodles!!

ALLIE

That big red door at Shanghai Winter Palace, to pick up shrimp toasts, egg roll, black bean fried rice, that egg drop soup you like, and, yes, your peanut-sesame noodles, but they wouldn't answer! God knows they're probably so scared . . . can you imagine being a Chinese in this? I mean, it's not like it's *their* fault, they're from goddamn San Gabriel, they didn't bring the—the—the virus?

JAPHY

They did not indeed bring it here. In point of fact, some fucking asshole skiers from Encino did, direct from Livigno in northern fucking Italy.

ALLIE

Exactly. The Woons, they're not guilty. I stood there, and I said, "Mr. Woon, I'm not here for trouble, I just want an egg roll or a sizzling rice soup." Jesus, nothing. Didn't get a goddamn thing!

JAPHY

Could be time to give up on LA, Allie. Thank God you haven't gotten rid of my car.

ALLIE

Your car? Dad's ole Caddy station wagon? Dad always knew just what to do, get us all in and go up to Tahoe or Yosemite. Pack sandwiches. He was a diamond in the rough. Just don't talk about Nixon. He loved that man and hated hippies.

JAPHY

He sure did love that fuckin' car. Man. Emerald green with leather seats. I could not believe he gave it to you—

ALLIE

You were a hippie, right, Japhy? Irresponsible. Couldn't take care of yourself, couldn't take care of the Caddy!

JAPHY

He was far too tough. An unkind bastard, really. I mean . . . c'mon. Mom . . .

ALLIE

Not a *fancy pants* Jewish guy. Thick arms. Worker's arms. Never could find a guy like that.

Sunlight washes over Japhy, dust motes in air obscure him.

JAPHY

Not a nice man. But. He gave *you* things. And you took them. Every single one of them.

ALLIE

I knew how to finesse him! Unlike you! Those guys, old-fashioned guys. Took care of things. People today. Talk. Talk. Talk. Dad walked the talk.

JAPHY

Yeah, people talk more today than they ever fucking have, babe.

ALLIE

Today, you say *one wrong thing*, not even *knowing*. I mean Mom, she used to say, "Okay, lets get *Oriental*" on any given Sunday. "Oriental." Or "Negro" this or that.
 (*beat*)
She would wave at me with her chopsticks, with a mouth full of moo shu pork, and say, "Please, Allie, pass me the Oriental plum sauce. Pass me the Oriental slippery shrimp . . ." And she didn't mean anything mean or racist by it. Well—today—if you even—

ALLIE *at the phone—dials from memory. Puts it on speaker.*

JAPHY

Who you callin'? Twin Dragon might be open. They
have those nice shumai dumplings with shrimp, very . . .
calming.

The phone rings, and then . . .

MR. STILL (ON SPEAKER)

*You have reached Nick Stein Pharmacy. We can't answer
the phone right now as we are with other customers.
Please press pound and wait for the beep and leave a
detailed message for the pharmacy.*

She presses # and there is a BEEP.

ALLIE

This is like Venezuela! It's Allie Murchow, and this is
the fourth message I've left. I don't know what to say.
I'm trying to find Touche Éclat pens and a refill of
my essential medication. Please call me back. CrestView
6-5969—

MR. STILL (ON SPEAKER)

—Hello! Hello?

Lights on MR. STILL *at a phone stand in the pharmacy. Young,
slim, handsome, and well-dressed, with thick black glasses.*

[29]

ALLIE

YES!!!!!

(astonished)

Hello? Are you— Oh my God, a *person*. *A person!*

MR. STILL

Hello? What can I do for you?

ALLIE

It's Alice—Allie—*Murchow*. Oh my God, I've been trying to reach you. I left word about my Respiridone script, from Dr. Wexler, and I tried to get over there to pick it up. But the streets are crazy with crowds of protestors—

MR. STILL

Birthday? . . .

ALLIE

My birthday? Why do you— Oh—okay—okay—it's—

(beat)

June four, 1950. The day *In a Lonely Place* was released, and my mother was at the movies—

MR. STILL

Esther *Murrow* on Rexford Drive? I'm not showing us filling anything. You said Dr. Wexler called it in? *Barry* Wexler or— Or Carla Wexler the ortho—

ALLIE

(snaps)

Murchow! *No*, I'm not on Rexford! I'm 815 South
Sherbourne Drive, unit 202! Not *Barry* Wexler, that's his
brother. They don't even *talk*, he's a radiologist *for God's
sake*, Dr. *Hy* Wexler, the . . . the psychopharmacologist
on Roxbury Drive—

MR. STILL

Murchow, Murchow, Murchow, Wexler, Hy, Wexler Hy,
no—there's a Weller and a Hy Waxman . . . could it be
under any other name? You *sure* he called it in? What
was it? Resperidone?

ALLIE

(certain)

Yes, Resperidone! Yes, he promised he was going to.
He—where is Nick Stein? I need to talk to Nick or
Louise!

MR. STILL

Ms. Murchow, Nick or Louise have not been here for a
very long time—

ALLIE

(snaps over him)

I was being rhetorical, like "where is Nick?" *He* knew
me, kind of thing!!! Listen: M-U-R and "chow" like the

dog or eating or the restaurant Mr. Chow. One block from you! Mur-chow. Wait, who is this? Is this Len? Is Len there?

MR. STILL

I'm Spencer *Still*—

ALLIE
(excited)

I know you! Spencer? You went to Beverly Hills High and played badminton—were you at my birthday party at Kiddieland with the *helicopter ride*?

MR. STILL
(bewildered)

No, that's some other Spencer. Hold on.
(calls off)
Hey, anybody filling a script for an Allie—or Alice— Mur-chow, a Dr. *Hy* Wexler, not Barry. Hy! She said he called it in? Anyone?
(snaps to someone off)
Mister, you're gonna have to wait. No, we don't have any *pure* alcohol. Nobody does! Clorox? Clorox for *what*? I'm sorry I'm dealing with another— Hey!! Hold on please!!
(to ALLIE*)*
It's nuts here. Sorry, Ms. Murrow—

ALLIE

That's not my name. It's Murchow.

MR. STILL

(to someone else; sirens)

Jesus Christ. What do you mean the police are *closing* all of Beverly Hills? Are you kidding me? A curfew?

ALLIE	MR. STILL
They're *closing*—Beverly Hills??? *How?* Oh. My GOD.	—I'm gonna put you on hold for a minute.

ALLIE

No! No. Please! No, no, no—

Now helicopters. Circling.

MR. STILL

I'll be right back, I promise. You can hold or call back—

ALLIE

(desperate)

I'll hold! No. NO! I'll hold.

ALLIE *goes to a remote for a small flat TV mounted in her kitchen, turns it on.*

TOM SELLECK (VOICE ON TV)

"This isn't my first rodeo. And let me tell you something: I wouldn't be here if I thought reverse mortgages took advantage of any American senior."

ALLIE *snaps off the TV.*

MR. STILL

Listen, Ms. Murchow, so, it's true, we have to close early. The protestors are coming into Beverly Hills.

ALLIE

Listen, you've got to help me, please, Spencer. I mean, even if it's just a few pills, okay?

MR. STILL

Can you get here by three? I mean. And we have to reach your doctor too. Dr. Wexler?
(to someone off)
Hey, hold on! No, look, there's a line! There's—yes, I know it's—Mr. Mizlansky, we have your script, it's ready!

ALLIE

Listen, Spencer, I was out there. They are protesting already right *here*. Pico and Robertson. I don't know why . . . why here? Do they think people like me, decent people, are on the side of the sick cops who did things like that? I got yelled at and shoved to the ground!

MR. STILL

I know. It's not good out there. I know.
(beat)
. . . Ms. Murrow, do you have a phone number for Dr. Wexler?

ALLIE

Just a second. Okay. Sure. You'd think I'd know it.
(Looks at address book. It is very old. Yellow pages
fall out.)
CrestView 6-4275 . . . He's at the Roxbury Medical Building. Suite 304.

MR. STILL

Okay . . . Ms. Murchow. Uhm . . .
(suddenly gentle, dealing with someone with issues)
. . . And you've filled the prescription here with us? Before? You're certain?

ALLIE

(on the verge of tears)
I am. I am. Yes. I don't *have* another pharmacy. I would never have another pharmacy, ever. Mr. Stein brought antibiotics and pain meds and pastilles to the house when I was a kid with God knows what, and when we

came in, he gave me extra British candy at the front counter! Cadbury violet flake. I just saw him! I just saw *him*!!! At Roxbury Park, walking his dog, Chestie, and they waved at me!

MR. STILL

Let me check again.

JAPHY *appears. We hear protestors chanting outside.*

JAPHY

It's getting pretty interesting out there, Alicious!

ALLIE

They are making an already fucked-up situation even worse!

JAPHY

Yeah, they are making it worse. For people like *you*!

ALLIE

Like me? I walked the walk. I was at the original, the original Equal Rights March in Washington. I went! Two gals in my book club are Black, for Christ's sake—

MR. STILL

Okay, Ms. Murchow. Resperidone. Can you tell me *why* this was prescribed?

JAPHY

Because you're hopelessly out of touch? Or because you're hopelessly batshit crazy?

MR. STILL

(to someone else)

Hey, leave me alone, okay? I'm helping this lady. I have to help her, it's a situation, okay?

(back to phone)

Ms. Murchow, can you tell me what the medication is prescribed for?

JAPHY

Tell him it's for panic attacks.

ALLIE

It is for . . . calming.

JAPHY

It's for severe anxiety.

ALLIE

It is for clear thinking. It helps with peace of mind, for people who have anxiety issues, which, in my case, are stabilized.

JAPHY

Really? Respiridone; brand name Risperdal, anti-psychotic medication.

ALLIE

It soothes. A magic bullet for me, I gotta tell you.

MR. STILL

And . . . when was your last dose?

ALLIE

When? I guess a while ago.

MR. STILL

So . . . You ran out? And do you know when?

ALLIE

I can't be sure of the—the exact time . . .

MR. STILL
(gentle)

I see. I'm going to put you on hold for a moment and see if we can get to the bottom of this, okay?

ALLIE

Okay. Okay. Okay.

JAPHY
(great idea!)

Allie? How 'bout we make an olive oil polenta lemon cake? Drench it in Campari, bake it, have some Stilton, a small salad with pears, and then the *cake*!

ALLIE

(furious)

I don't have *Campari*! *Campari*? Japhy. Please. What do
you think this is: La Scala?

JAPHY

(feigned innocence)

Jeez, no need to snap. You maybe . . . are maybe mad at
me about something.

ALLIE

About what?

JAPHY

The past . . . drugs and things . . .

ALLIE

Oh. Well, I mean, look what it did to you. You destroyed
your lungs. You *still* smoke.

JAPHY

Not the fucking cigarettes. I put you in a position to care
for me when you were in no condition to help anyone—

ALLIE

No, stop it. If you start this now, then I send you back to
your part of the apartment, okay, Japhy? I mean it, not
now!!

JAPHY	MR. STILL
(grins)	*(suddenly on the phone)*
My "*part*" of the apartment? Now that's funny. Now that's— yeah—okay, my "part." Ooph. Wow.	. . . Hello, Ms. Murchow. So maybe *you* can check, see if you can find Dr. Wexler and have him call it in?

ALLIE

Yes! Yes, good idea!

MR. STILL

Look. Call this number: 310-274-4912. It's my direct line. I'll pick up here. See if you can reach him before the curfew, and we'll fill your prescription. Okay?

ALLIE
(so relieved)
You're so *kind*. I really appreciate it—
(flirty)
And you have a really cute voice—

JAPHY

Oh my God, please, get real! Don't do sex kitten—

ALLIE
(gestures to shut up)
I bet you're just adorable. Are you sure we haven't met? I came in a few days ago for those—the little leather

house slippers with the heel, the support, you got from
France.

JAPHY

You are such a fucking slattern!

ALLIE
(calm)

I'll reach Dr. Wexler, don't you worry. He was my
brother's doctor. He was the psychopharmacologist
for all of us, even when my father fell apart when the
studio let him go and my mom got fired from the
costume department at Metro. You're really a doll,
Spencer. I mean it. Thanks.

She hangs up. He does too.

MR. STILL

Good *Lord*. Does anyone know this woman, Alice
Murchow?

ALLIE *looks at the yellowed pages of the phone book. Dials
phone.*

WOMAN'S VOICE

*You've reached the exchange for Roxbury Drive Medical
Partners. Nobody is available to take your call, but please
leave a message. Press one for Dr. Cho, two for Canyon*

Cosmetic Surgery Group, three for Dr. Siberell, four for Dr. Weller, and five for general messages.

BEEP. ALLIE *presses 4.*

ALLIE

Dr. *Wexler.* They may have said "Weller."

(to phone)

This is Allie Murchow. Leaving word. I think there's been a mix-up; you were gonna call in my meds to Nick Stein and I— They don't have it. Can you call me and them back? Boy, these riots are shaking me up. So inconsiderate of older people, of people who are not well! March on City Hall if you wanna march!! Please! Do they not know that the Jewish people have always stood side by side by the Black people? I was at a fundraiser at The Bistro Garden for some Black Panther who went to Cuba or Monrovia. This would be 1974. Cody took me because Shirley MacLaine—

JAPHY

I fucking took you. Not stupid Cody.

ALLIE

When I think of how Jewish people always . . . we always were there for the cause of equality. And now *this*? This? I think it's time for a phone session—or even better, I could come in and see you.

(beat)

Can you hear out my window? So much anger. So much anger in the world now. And not with the right people, am I right? Okay. So. I'll wait for a call back. Thanks, honey.

She hangs up. Protestors. She moves to the refrigerator. Takes out two eggs and arugula and chops. Breaks eggs, seasons, puts butter in pan, and makes quick omelette. JAPHY *comes into the kitchen.*

JAPHY

Allie. I think maybe it's not actually appropriate to call one's psychiatrist *honey.*

ALLIE
(ignores him)
Do you *hear* them? All because of *one bad cop. One* bad. *One!* A thousand miles from here!

JAPHY
(a laugh)
Oh baby, more than one. You know that.

ALLIE
I was background on the police movie *The New Centurions* starring George C. Scott, who was a doll—

JAPHY

Don't you mean *Stacy Keach* was a doll?

ALLIE

Yes. Yes. Stacy *Keach* was a doll on that shoot, *not* Scott. And I got to talk to some of them, the police who worked that shoot. One of them—hah! We went on a date, we went to the Smoke House in Burbank. He was so macho and not Jewish. Oscar Maldonado was his name. We dated for about a month. Not a nice guy, rough, mean . . .

JAPHY

Kinda like Dad . . .

ALLIE

Wanted me to move to San Pedro, take care of two kids from a previous marriage, and I had a career! I know a little about bad cops!

JAPHY

Yeah, bad cops.

(beat)

Look, Allie, listen to me: Something is coming, and there needs to be some way for you to be prepared for it. I remember this thing. I remember Steve McQueen, he told me on his very last picture. He said, "Stunt Boy"—he called me Stunt Boy—and he said—

ALLIE

One step from stardom but always *high*! Steve McQueen's stunt double. HIGH!

JAPHY

Don't interrupt, Christ! McQueen. He said after the night of the Manson murders everyone bought a gun the next day, all the liberals, they bought gorgeous little nine-millimeter pistolas for their pockets and shit, and he said, "Stunt Boy, they finally got it. 'Be prepared for what's to come!'" Allie, you must prepare for the reckoning. I don't see much preparation. And it's coming . . . shit. It's already here. Right here. Right now!!

ALLIE *pours a glass of white wine. She dumps the omelet.*

ALLIE

Are you suggesting I should leave LA and get a gun?

JAPHY

That's what you got from that?

ALLIE

No. NO! I won't give up on Los Angeles.

JAPHY

But it's already given up on *you*. It's given up on all the things it used to be, babe. "The horizontal light, the low buildings, the alleys, and the taco stands." That's why those people out there are *mad*. Everybody protested the buildings shaped like fucking hot dogs disappearing. They protested that shit, but not that life was not right for those people out there, life was out of joint for them. And of course *you* don't, you won't see that, will you, dear, dear Allie Murchow! You won't see it, and you won't see me—because it gets in the way of the makeup and the hair color . . .

JAPHY *exits down the hall into darkness.* ALLIE *downs the wine, helicopters hover, and she turns on her TV—a CoverGirl makeup ad can be heard with an electronic beat as lights fade on* ALLIE.

COVERGIRL AD LADY
"Looking for a smoky eye that's subtle enough for day and dramatic enough for night? Look no further than the nudes eye palette from CoverGirl—first apply creme to the brow bone. Then, using TruNaked liner—"

BLACKOUT.

[SCENE III]

"In Everything That's Light and Gay"

A day later.

Piercing LA white light, dizzyingly, dazzlingly blinding.
Particulate matter floating and refracting in the sunlight,
filling the air.

ALLIE straightens up the house. She's wearing mid-'90s
Marni pants and shirt, secondhand, but hers. Lots of
Lucite jewelry.

She is on hold with Nick Stein Pharmacy again. "I'll Be
Seeing You" plays. JAPHY is napping on the couch in very
old, faded jeans and a plain gray T-shirt. ALLIE is riffing on
"I'll Be Seeing You."

ALLIE
(singing)

I'll be seeing you
In all the goddamn places
That this heart of mine embraces

All day through
In that Oriental place
The market across the way
More Chinese food,
The Trader Joe's
The striptease shows
I'll be seeing you
In every lovely Ross Dress for Less
In everything that's light and gay
The whole damn town is gay!
I'll always think of you that way
Cody, you went to the wrong
Du-par's. I'll be looking at my bed
and I'll be seein' you
Cody dah dee dah doo—

There is a loud BEEP.

MR. STILL

Uhm, Ms. Murchow?

LIGHTS ON. MR. STILL *in his little pharmacy setting.*

ALLIE

Hi, Spencer?

MR. STILL

See, I think . . . look, is there anyone I can— Is there
anyone else there with you to talk to?

JAPHY

How 'bout me?

ALLIE

No. Well, my brother, but he has strep throat.

ALLIE *glares at the still grinning* JAPHY.

MR. STILL

See, okay . . . well. The thing is, your Dr. Wexler. I did
some research, and he retired and—

ALLIE

He retired without *telling* me?

MR. STILL

Uhm. Ms. Murchow . . . Dr. Wexler—I am really
sorry to be the one telling you this, but he's . . . he's
dead—

ALLIE

He *died*? How? How did he? What happened?

MR. STILL
(helpless)

Well. Look. He died some time ago. So. Did you run out
of your prescription a while ago?

ALLIE

No. Look. Hon. You have the wrong Wexler, baby.

That must be his brother, *Barry*, the brother was much older. This is Dr. *Hy* Wexler at the Roxbury Medical—

MR. STILL

Yes. Hy Wexler is buried at Westwood Cemetery. I'm reading his obituary online. He died two years ago.

JAPHY

Ohhhh. Okay. So that happened!

ALLIE

Oh. Okay. You know what? That's a *good* cemetery. Natalie Wood is there. I think Elizabeth Montgomery is there, too.

JAPHY

Marilyn is there—

MR. STILL

. . . Do you have another doctor I could call?

ALLIE

I have the gynecologist at Kaiser? I have to look her up. Dr. Amarian, I think.

MR. STILL

I mean another *psychiatrist*?

ALLIE

The—the—the breast . . . What's her name? What's her name? She's very big. Big breast surgeon. I think you're—you're new there, right? So you don't know her?

MR. STILL

I've been working here for three years. The last thing we have for you on record is some Ativan from 2015, and before that Elavil. I think I've seen you come in for makeup sometimes and—

ALLIE

Yes, yes, so you *do* know me?! I come in for makeup and . . . and my meds . . . and my meds, and I can't have generic!

MR. STILL

Ms. Murchow—

ALLIE

You do know me! So the Repsoridel. You can give it to me now. And the CoverGirl for smoky eye—

MR. STILL

No. No, I can't—I am very sorry. I would like to speak with your primary care physician, please.

ALLIE

Okay. You listen to me right now—

JAPHY

Blow it all up! No prep for the reckoning—Blow It Up!

JAPHY *heads into the bedroom.*

ALLIE

I don't like what is going on. I don't like this. And you
know what? Fine. I don't need your Respicalore.
                    (quietly furious)
I don't need it. Because there's meditation and
breathing, and those drugs make you gain weight
anyway. Tuesday Weld! Look at her! I mean, it's not
right to do this to someone. It's called *gaslighting*, did
you know that? I could report you! I want to speak to—
                        (a yell)
A Stein! Nicky, or Lou, or Chita, or . . .

MR. STILL

Ms. Murchow, there are no members of the Stein
family here. Are you still at 815 South Sherbourne,
apartment 202?

DORSA	ALLIE
(from off)	Yes, I am. You gonna
Allie? Allie?	bring over the meds?

MR. STILL

I just want to know, because if you need help, I will—

[52   ]

ALLIE

I don't like this game you're playing.

The front door opens. DORSA *carries a tray of food.*

DORSA

. . . Allie?

ALLIE

Dorsa, they don't *know* me at Nick Stein Pharmacy! Can you imagine?

MR. STILL

Look, I think we have to do something to help you. Did someone just come in? Can I talk to them?

ALLIE *hangs up the phone.*

ALLIE

(to DORSA*)*

That man was making threats to me. Pretending to be a Stein.

DORSA

Look! I brought you the Persian pomegranate stew you like. Fesenjan chicken stew.

ALLIE

You're such a sweetie. I really need this food. Right now. Thank God. I can't get anyone to come here. For food delivery. For medicines. Not anyone.

(*food on the table*)

Oh, it smells so good.

DORSA

Pomegranates, walnuts, and organic chicken.

ALLIE

I haven't eaten today. Yesterday Shanghai Winter wouldn't open up for delivery. Kosher Chinese, what a terrible combination. The virus and the protestors, *another* terrible combination! Scary times, Dorsa.

DORSA *sits across from* ALLIE.

DORSA

Well, I don't blame them for not delivering, and I don't blame the protestors either.

ALLIE

(*eating*)

Oh, this is good. Neighbors are good. I'm so tired of all the anger out there.

DORSA

My darling, they have lots to be angry about.

ALLIE

(eating)

Meh, who doesn't? Everyone has a story.

DORSA

Let's not start to compare—

ALLIE

You think *I'm* so happy? My hours were cut at Neiman Marcus down to nada, baby. And *you*?

Kicked out of your country by the—the Khomeini and that crowd of winners. Believe me, who *isn't* angry? Everybody has something to be angry about. Do you know . . . Dr. Wexler, my old doctor, *died* and nobody tells me! And he's buried in Westwood Cemetery!

(eats)

Why couldn't the protestors wait till there was a vaccine? The vaccine is coming, the president said it is, the vaccine comes and *then* you protest, then gather and speak out!

DORSA

The police are killing Black people *now*, my dear. So there *is* no more waiting. That little kid, Dewy, from downstairs? Beaten by police for wearing a hoodie, for walking alone in the middle of the afternoon. From school. Police said they couldn't see his face—

ALLIE

Yes, yes. But too much disruption. The—the—I hate him, this president, but he's right. The president—he's right about too much happening too quick. I hate him, but things need to seriously slow down—

DORSA

(cuts her off)

He is hateful. And he is racist. Black mothers cannot safely send their children off to school—they live in fear. Afraid of police and MAGA people!

ALLIE

Please. I'm on their side! The Black mothers! I also believe in reparations! Look, six friends from my Holocaust book club, I kicked them out for insisting on discussing how great the president is. I do my part! But the fact is, this disruption is in my neighborhood. This danger is directed toward me . . . AND I DON'T LIKE IT!

DORSA

We *must* be disrupted! Look, you've got to break some eggs to make an omelet, believe me!

ALLIE

I made an omelet yesterday but couldn't even eat it. I don't want to talk about the politics, really . . . the politics of it. No more.

DORSA

Allie, this is the test of your lifetime! It is! Do not turn away! You must face it!

ALLIE

(thinks for a second)

You know, I told you about Cody, my ex. Well, we used to go to this place called Lucky's in Montecito, when we stayed at the Biltmore. They had a steak and a chilled crabmeat cocktail. We—he—had money then. He was on a show called *The Rookies* for a season or two. I think three. He was this cute cop, Cody, his character was named Bing, but they killed his character finally when the ratings slipped. He had a dreamy little Porsche, a house in Laurel Canyon. You know, Cody lost that *Rookies* job and had to go to Vegas just to survive. But I know he's somewhere out there! Waiting for me. Probably.

DORSA

Listen: Take a shower. Put on a nice outfit. We will walk to the park and back. You need some fresh air and sunshine.

ALLIE

It's not safe out there.

DORSA

Just to La Cienega . . . or we can go to Westwood
Cemetery and visit your Dr. Wexler.

ALLIE

Look, the mob—you can't get to the stars or Dr. Wexler.
Where even is Elizabeth Montgomery buried? She was
so nice—

DORSA

I'll hold your arm, you'll be okay. We don't even have
to walk. We can take an Uber or even the bus to
Westwood.

ALLIE

Okay, well . . . do you have some Xanax? I ran out—

DORSA

I'm not going to give you medication. You don't want to
be sick again! Do you?

ALLIE

Please, Dorsa, don't interrogate me.

DORSA

We are women. And we are neighbors. And you are on
a fixed income, and I am a person of color. We have to
look out for each other no matter what! In this country,

neighbors do not look out for each other. They look out for themselves.

So NO BULLSHIT! Me and Rupert upstairs and Schneider from 2-C are looking out for you.

ALLIE

I don't like this.

DORSA

We've seen what happens with you.

ALLIE

What happens with me, Dorsa?

DORSA

I saw it in Tehran in 1979! I said to Rostam, "Don't just sit there and hide. Get up, get moving! To be a Jew in Iran now is impossible! Time to be strong and fight!" Rostam folded up, Allie. He could not cope with the changes. He froze, and then broke. This is what is happening in America now! You cannot hide and break, Allie!

ALLIE

What would help is if I could redecorate. I was planning on doing new closets and new slipcovers. That hasn't been redone since the 1988 season.

DORSA

New slipcovers? This is not the way to live a life! I am
volunteering at Cedars-Sinai twice a week. I go in there.
You stay cooped up in here, forgive me. Yes, you look
gorgeous, your makeup is perfect, but please, what are
you doing?

ALLIE

Yes, I get caught up . . . but I'm busy.

DORSA

Everyone in the building is now worried about you.

ALLIE

All the people? And so they sent you?

DORSA

We *care* about you. We are all in this together—
neighbors. But Allie, you have to have a reason. A
reason to live. A purpose.

ALLIE
(whispers)
I take care of my brother! That is a purpose!

DORSA

Allie. Please, this is not healthy . . . and this is not
reality!

(pained truth)

Your brother's care. It was never you. It was me.

ALLIE

Uh-huh. I know you mean well, Dorsa. Would you mind now if I asked you to leave? I have so much to do. So much housework.

DORSA

Really? Do you, Allie?

ALLIE

Yes. I have to dust my artifacts. And I have to call them back at Nick Stein Pharmacy.

DORSA

(challenging)

You want me to leave?

ALLIE

I have a lot to do here. I am not being rude, I just . . . the fires made dust everywhere. My father's award for film cutting from his union and . . . and he was one of the last negative cutters in the business. Did you know that? So . . . you need to leave. Sometimes you have to draw a line.

ALLIE *opens the front door and gestures for* DORSA *to leave.*

DORSA

Okay, my dear.

ALLIE

And. May I please have my key back?

DORSA

You want your *key*?

ALLIE

I am not comfortable with—

DORSA
(strong and clear)
For now. I shall keep it.

DORSA *exits.* ALLIE *dials phone.*

MR. STILL

You have reached Spencer Still at Nick Stein Pharmacy. We are closed early because of the curfew. Please leave me a message after the tone. I will get back to you as quickly as I can.

A BEEP.

ALLIE

Hello, Spencer. Can you pick up? Hello? Please. Mr. Still? Please pick up. I'm so sorry for hanging up on you. I was very upset. My Persian neighbor was upsetting me. You just have to set limits with people. I have trouble with that. So. Please call me back. Thank you, honey. Stay safe.

Dust fills the room.

BLACKOUT.

[SCENE IV]

"I'll Be Looking at the Moon"

As lights up—"La Mer"—the Julio Iglesias version of this song is on the stereo. JAPHY *is in a suit from the 1970s, a very good one, very Warren Beatty in* Shampoo. *He is drinking champagne.* ALLIE *is in a YSL pantsuit, also drinking.*

ALLIE
(roaring with laughter)
—he went to the wrong fucking Du-par's!

JAPHY
(laughs)
Oh yeah, I know the whole story, man. Okay, I know it.
Poor fuckin' Cody, you yellin' at him into the goddamn
phone. Then the breakdown and Cedars. You wouldn't
see him. He was a nice guy. I liked him. Short little
fucker, like a bantam rooster, but he sure could dance.
Remember we went to that theater?

ALLIE
La Mirada Civic Theatre! He—he was in, what was it? *A
Salute to Broadway*!!

JAPHY

(singing brightly, parody of showy sparkle)

"Ohh there's trouble, trouble in River City." Corny bullshit, but the man could dance. He had a very light foot. Very light. Come on, let's dance, Allie.

They dance and have fun.

ALLIE

This was such a good idea. Dress-up party. Escape. Fun. Dance. You . . . one thing you always have been good at . . . finding the fun.

JAPHY

Yeah, you needed this, Allie. Forgive, forget, and live!!!

ALLIE

(laugh)

Yeah. Who goes to the wrong Du-par's? When did anyone go over the hill to the Valley to that Du-par's?

JAPHY

Yeah, ahh. That was a big one for you, Allie. Man, you really—wow—Cody—you got dressed, you put on some, like, purple velvet thingie. You were a fox that night. Du-par's—not exactly the Polo Lounge or the Daisy.

ALLIE

(dances to the music)

Ahh, remember the Daisy on Rodeo! Sinatra flirted
with me. He was there with Mia and wanted to take me
home.

*Silence for a moment. JAPHY nods. His tone shifts. Slower,
deeper into the booze and late hour.*

JAPHY

Yeah. No, he didn't. He was into Mia, okay? I wish you
wouldn't do that—pretend these guys were into you.
You have such a problem with that shit. These fantasies
about who was into you, man. Warren. Stacy. Michael
Ontkean. All the men who loved you, from Dad to Nick
Stein.

ALLIE

Oh please! Come on . . . when you weren't doing stunts,
you were in the bars with the boys, okay? You weren't
exactly a stable family man, ever! Who is the escape
artist? Which of us? We both—

JAPHY

Were weak. Why? My God, what happened to make us
both so broken? Tell me, Allie!!

ALLIE

What you did to yourself, what you did to your own
lungs, smoking that white crack . . .

JAPHY

(breaks in)

LOVE. It's *love* fucked us both, isn't it? My dreams . . .
touching, being touched, just someone touch me, some
man, some guy slightly more than me, more. Slightly
more everything than me. Please touch me.

I remember saying that over and over at the gym,
at school, surfing, or to some actor who thought I was
his bud. And when I found it, I ran and then kept on
looking for it—

ALLIE

That is why I went to meet Cody that night, okay? The
night. I needed to be touched too.

JAPHY

Except Cody went to the wrong place. Why? No more
make-believe.

ALLIE

Cody was a scatterbrain! He fucked up! Simple as
that!

JAPHY

Okay. So. Let's think about that. You so overreacted to his small, understandable fuckup? Screaming into the phone at Du-par's after he called to tell you he was sorry—but you in your velvet suit. Why did you go so berserk that night?

ALLIE

Oh, okay. Stunt Boy!! You're so smart, tell me!

JAPHY

Du-par's! You went to tell Cody, "Japhy will be gone soon, and I'm so tired! I've worked so hard, given so much, his body is failing him. Cody, it's time for a fresh start. Us. A life together."

ALLIE

You never had the anxiety I did. I had to put on a show just to get outta here. Baby, you have no idea how hard it was for me to be in here with you.

JAPHY

I *heard you* rehearsing at your precious vanity! Rehearsing your sorrow: "Mom and dad gone, the last of the Murchows. I am the Last. Of. The. Line. A Jew wandering into nothingness, a bloodline dying out. Cody, I cannot sacrifice any longer."

(beat)

Is that the basic sense of it, Allie?

ALLIE

Your whole *life*. Of sex in alleyways. Your hepatitis. A, B, and C. Your broken limbs from stunts, your HIV, your survival and survival and survival when your body told you to give it up—*Do you know how hard that anxiety is?* Watching you hold on to—what?

JAPHY

Look at you, always arguing for your special status as the great fucking victim, the one for whom no task is easy, pleading your emotional handicaps prevent you, as much as you might like, from helping your own brother—

ALLIE

I didn't have your confidence! I saw everything, every flaw, every blemish in my skin. Mom looking at me and saying, "Maybe you can do character work, but you're not a star," and Dad, "Don't get your hopes up, you'll always be a cutter." And me, my hair color wrong, my nose the wrong shape.

JAPHY

Your wrong nose and your wrong hair color were the reason I died that night. You ran out of here, in my last

[70]

hours, and went to Du-par's to beg for a new life. With Cody?

ALLIE

You had it so much easier! A boy with confidence and looks! You shoulda been the strong one. Shoulda been the man!

JAPHY

And isn't that why Cody went to the wrong Du-par's? He saw how you abandoned me! He knew! And didn't wanna deal with Allie when she stopped needing him, when it required sacrifice! A selfless LOVE! So basically, he wanted to hit the road to Vegas, to come up with dance numbers for Shirley and the gang. So much easier! Than Allie Murchow! That's why he went to the wrong goddamn Du-par's. Because he knew you would not go the distance!

ALLIE

I should never have offered to care for you. It was too much for me. No—not home hospice care.

JAPHY

Allie. It was home hospice care *in my own fucking home.*

ALLIE

But I did it. Because you'd have been in a horrible facility. In a shared room, washed by some stranger.

Let me tell you a little secret. *Dorsa* washed me. *Dorsa* held my hand. *Dorsa* sang to me. I was happy to die in front of Dorsa rather than in front of you. Dying in front of *you* would have been a tremendous strain on you (and me, for that fucking matter). It is hard work, dying, babe. It is embarrassing and private, but Dorsa has seen so much of it. She was built for it, and you were not. For her, it was an act of love. Love the neighbor as the self. For real.

(beat)

And when Cody didn't show? What then? What was it like when you finally got back here after seventy-two hours in the Cedars psych ward?

ALLIE
(defiant to the end)

I painted. Your room. I gave away the cowboy boots and the records. I threw away the sex toys and the detective novels and the cowboy poetry and the sailing books and the surfing books and your Oxford OED, I created a clean and empty . . .

JAPHY
(bitter)

Future.

ALLIE

Apartment. And I felt . . . RELIEF. I had survived.

JAPHY

Survived . . . me. The "me" who was fucking sick.

ALLIE

I had to think of myself. You drained every last inch
of—

JAPHY
(over her)

I carried you across *all* the finish lines, didn't I? Bol-
stering, hoisting, lifting. Across Dad, Mom, Elizabeth
Montgomery! All your suffering and limitations, and
you couldn't give me a little care.

(beat; ALLIE *is silent)*

Then COVID, and the chaos hits the streets, so you
call all the old phone numbers of all your old helpers.
The Nick Steins, mom and dad, the Dr. Wexlers,
and me!

(a gentle and quiet truth)

Your fear and anxiety. Not my problem! I lived my life.
I paid for my pleasures. You pay for yours in your way,
but don't make me into your Stations of the Cross, baby,
okay?

That's not my jam. I ain't in the expiation business,
sister! *I want out!*

And silence.

ALLIE

Well . . . The protestors are gone now.

JAPHY

(a sly smile)

I still hear some of them out there. Out in the night.
By that ugly pool. Under the palm. Waiting. Are they
waiting *for you*?

ALLIE

(flat)

And why would they wait for me?

JAPHY

They recognize the real problem is you. What'd you
ever, for instance, take responsibility for? Not for them.
And certainly not for me. Only you. The you that hates
what they ask for. Respect, reciprocity, regard . . . at
some possible cost to your infinite, infinite comfort.
Your comfort.

ALLIE

Totally ridiculous!

JAPHY

Nice. You're someone who thinks they're nice.

ALLIE

Stop. Please stop!

JAPHY
(*Clear. Crisp. Ice*)

You, Allie, are a coldhearted, thoughtless, selfish bitch. Who actually knows it, but hides behind the makeup and the fragility and the fake ditziness in hopes that someone might feel sorry, pity even, and give *you* something unearned.

Stunned silence from ALLIE. *She holds out her hand. A gesture of* Don't you say anything more!

Silence. There is a BUZZ over the intercom.

MR. STILL (INTERCOM)

Ms. Murchow, it's Spencer Still. From Nick Stein Pharmacy. Ms. Murchow?

ALLIE
(*totally shaken*)

Uhm, Nick Stein? *Finally?* Are you kidding? Do you have my medication?

MR. STILL (INTERCOM)

Uhm, I—

ALLIE

Good. Come up, please. It's the door on the left up the stairs.

Jesus. You even got that kid to come over. You are the tenth wonder of the fucking Western, free-market world.

JAPHY *moves quietly into the shadows. A knock on the door.*

ALLIE

I'm coming!

ALLIE *opens door.* MR. STILL *is there in mask and baseball hat.*

MR. STILL

Hi. Ms. Murchow.

ALLIE

Please come in, thank you so much. Do you want some water? Or anything? Campari soda? You are a lifesaver! I knew I was in the system. My God, you got here, despite the curfew—

MR. STILL

Ms. Murchow, I don't have a prescription for you. I was just . . . I was worried about you.

ALLIE

I'm sorry, sweetie, I can't hear you with the mask. I'll
back up six feet, and you can take your mask off. So I
can see your cute face.

He takes off his hat and mask. She is stunned. He is Asian.

ALLIE

Wait— Are you from Shanghai Winter Palace with the
sesame noodles?

MR. STILL
(confused)

Uhm? No? Ms. Murchow. I just wanted to say, I
wanted . . . I wanted to help you. You see, I don't have
your prescription, because you have not got one or had
one for some time, and I just wanted to offer to help you.

ALLIE
(disoriented)

I don't know what you're saying. What did Nick say?
Did he say I don't have— Look, if I don't have the— I
can take the generic, if I have to. If *that's* the problem,
you see, it just might not agree with me and I can adjust
to it. *I can.* We can sort out the insurance later.

MR. STILL

Do you have any family, any friends, anyone who helps
you? Because I wanted to offer to take you perhaps to

UCLA to the hospital there so you can get the medicine you need, and the help you need. Ms. Murchow?

ALLIE

You want to take me to the hospital?

MR. STILL

I did pray.

ALLIE

For what?

MR. STILL

Not to ignore you. Not to pretend you were not in trouble. That you have not called me for the past day. I am the man you call. I prayed not to ignore what you need.

ALLIE

I need my medication and some YSL—

MR. STILL

At the pharmacy, the Stein family is gone. Long gone. It's now owned by a conglomerate from Holland, I think. They said to ignore you. The liability issues alone. To ignore you. And I asked my cousin who is a social worker what to do, and she said, "Leave it alone, it's not your problem. She could sue you just for showing up.

She could call the police. She could . . ." "She's not well,"
I said.

ALLIE

Where are the Stein family?

MR. STILL

Mostly dead.

ALLIE

All of them?

MR. STILL

Not all.

ALLIE

Are they at Westwood Cemetery too? The dead ones,
that is.

MR. STILL

My parents said, "Why do you care about this woman
who keeps calling?" And I said, "Because she is in pain."
(beat)
You see, my church . . . I—I am part of a church.

ALLIE

I'm Jewish. What are you talking about? *A church?*
Please!

MR. STILL

I am not here to try and convert you or . . . it's something very important. To us, to be of service. And I wanted to offer to get you the help you need. If I may.

ALLIE

To be of . . . service? A good neighbor . . . ?
(finally)
That is kind. I do get frightened sometimes.

MR. STILL

My church tends to ignore pain unless it is the pain of the congregants. Unless it is tied to some immigrant dogma about America and God and the old country and—Jesus who died for—some prejudice. But I heard you. In real, actual pain.
(beat)
In pharmacy school we were taught to help people, and so I had to come see if you were at least all right, to check on you, to offer—

DORSA *is in the doorway.*

MR. STILL

—just anything I could do. I don't think you're doing okay, and I think you need help to get back on track.

DORSA

Hello, young man. Is everything okay here? I'm Ms. Murchow's friend. I live next door.

ALLIE

I'm confused. Dorsa, this is the man from Micky Stein.
This is Dorsa Yerushalaim.

(to MR. STILL)

Did, by any chance, did you bring the YSL Touche
Éclat All-Over Brightening Concealer Pen, darling? In
Luminous Peach? I ran out of that too.

DORSA

Allie? I think we have bigger problems—

ALLIE

I ran out when I used to go into the sun. You could use
Luminous Almond.

(to MR. STILL)

You did bring me my things, so kind of you.

MR. STILL

I did. I brought . . . we had, uhm, yes.

MR. STILL reaches into his backpack and takes out a Touche
Éclat Concealer Pen.

ALLIE

Touche Éclat! See, I can't go into the sun anymore.
I already had one cancer. I was lucky. It wasn't deep. I
have the skin of a baby, don't I?

MR. STILL

It says sample, but it hasn't been used.

MR. STILL *hands her the pen.*

ALLIE
(hypnotized)

Oh my God. Thank you. And it's the Peach—

She goes to the vanity table and starts applying it. She starts to undo her wig.

MR. STILL

Ms. Murchow. I know this has been very hard for you. Would you let me do something to help?

ALLIE

The secret is to follow the line—

She ignores SPENCER *and* DORSA. DORSA *looks at* SPENCER.

MR. STILL
(to DORSA*; quiet)*

Ms. Yerushalaim?

DORSA

Dorsa.

MR. STILL

. . . I am from the pharmacy, and Ms. Murchow has been calling us, very upset, for days.

DORSA

I know.

MR. STILL

About a prescription. About a medicine that her doctor . . . He has been dead for two years, and I think Ms. Murchow is confused. So I wanted to . . . I'm sorry. I think she needs some kind of emergency assistance. I think she might be in the middle of a break of some kind.
                    (quietly but brave)
Is there anyone who can help her?

DORSA *regards him with a kindness she reserves for the innocent and the doomed.*

DORSA
(quietly)
We can help Ms. Murchow, young man. You and I. Right, Allie?

ALLIE

Ohhh . . . ohhh . . . No. Yes. No. I'd—I would very much appreciate it if you could help me, maybe, yes . . .

DORSA

Of course, my dear. What do you need?

From the shadows, quietly, almost echoing in the darkness.

JAPHY

Some air. Fresh air.

ALLIE

Oh. Some fresh air. But. I'm afraid to go out alone.

DORSA

We'll be with you. Where do you want to go?

JAPHY

Westwood . . . to the cemetery.

ALLIE

Young man, do you have a car? Because I would very much like to go to Westwood Cemetery. To see some people. Elizabeth Montgomery. And Eve Arden. And my lovely Farrah Fawcett. She would come in before the Golden Globes or the Governors Ball so I could do her face. She's buried there, and I want to visit my old friends. Okay?

MR. STILL

I do have my car here, yes.

ALLIE

Even . . . even Darryl F. Zanuck is there. He gave me my first shot. He told his son Dick to put me in the Stars of Tomorrow program. Could we go there?

DORSA

Yes, Allie.

ALLIE

I'm tired. I'm so fucking tired. And probably should move out of this neighborhood, out to Santa Monica, overlooking the water. To Ocean Avenue. A nice little apartment over the water, with those breezes and no goddamn protestors telling me I don't care, that I don't care, that I don't care at all!

(starts to put on protective gear—her ritual)

Who can care all the time anyway?

I have benign cysts. I have ingrown toenails. I have just enough money to get by every month. I don't have an agent, so how can I get seen for anything? Even a goddamn two-line part would help. Do you know what? I was friends with people who were older. They're all dying now. The older people who cared about me. So how the fuck am I supposed to pay attention to everything that matters to the angry people out there? I never hurt them! I never— Maybe I didn't do enough.

JAPHY *is interested in this, and he emerges from the back*

hall, impossibly handsome in an unstructured Armani suit
right out of American Gigolo.

JAPHY

Okay, keep going. "Didn't do enough." Follow that
thought.

ALLIE

. . . I didn't exactly. Consider. Who might be hurt by my
being comfortable?

*She is distraught, lost, quietly trying to hold together parts
of herself.* ALLIE *looks at* JAPHY, *who has put on Armani
sunglasses.*

MR. STILL

All of us are trying to—to—

DORSA

Account for ourselves. At least you are asking the right
questions.

ALLIE

I have never been . . . Do you know that? I have never
been to the part of the cemetery where my own mom and
dad are? And of course . . . oh, of course . . . of course . . .
          (she can barely speak; a small laugh)
Ohh. I went to George C. Scott's grave because he put
me in *The New Centurions*, but I never tried to find

[86]

Mom and Dad. So. I would very much like to see my mom and dad. I think it's time.

DORSA *exchanges a glance with* MR. STILL; *they nod.*

The apartment recedes and . . .

[SCENE V]

"When the Night Is New"

WESTWOOD CEMETERY. DAY.

ALLIE, DORSA, *and* MR. STILL *are in a corner of Westwood Cemetery, looking around.* DORSA *points.*

ALLIE

My parents. Mom and Dad. And . . . Oh, my . . . Japhy. Japhy? Oh. Japhy?

(quietly breaking)

My brother's here. Japhy's right here. I mean. I mean, you know, Dorsa. You were with him while I was at Du-par's, waiting. I wanted anything else—their pancakes, anything other than what was . . . in the back bedroom. Poor Japhy. All alone, black and blue and thinned out and sores and . . .

Japhy, you are right *here now* . . . and they even bought one for me. Next to them. This is my spot.

(points to the earth)

Mom and Dad. You did. Among all these stars. One for me too. I don't know or understand who or what we were in my family, or how we became who we were and what we were. What we— I'm the only one left. I think about that. The only one of us left. To have lived in California through so much . . . and . . . I'm alone now . . . and there's a fire somewhere, maybe LA is burning, maybe it's burning up.

And poor Japhy. Do you know . . . I did not even do an unveiling ceremony? The Jews do it a year after someone dies. You go, you unveil the headstone, you say something . . . and then they have a resting place forever . . . They have a destiny in the forever . . . I never . . . I never. Did it . . . for Japhy.

DORSA

You are here now. If you want to say something. I am sure it is never the wrong time to—

ALLIE

. . . Maybe too much time—too much time has passed for words. He never bought my words anyway.

MR. STILL

. . . I could say the Lord's Prayer? Our Father, who art in heaven, hallowed—

ALLIE

(a laugh)

No, Jesus! Shut the fuck up. Lord's prayer for a Jewish atheist Buddhist surfer stuntman gay boy from Hollywood? Please! Why do the God people do God so much, so loudly?

MR. STILL *manages a small smile, sanguine, and perhaps touched that* ALLIE *is teasing him.*

DORSA

. . . Maybe this. I would sing this to Japhy to get him to sleep.

DORSA *briefly sings a verse in Persian, some sort of folk song.*

And JAPHY *appears. They see each other.*

DORSA

. . . We will leave you with your family. Come, Mr. Still.

DORSA *and* MR. STILL *wander off.*

Lights slowly fade to a red dusk glow on ALLIE *and* JAPHY.
To the east, the sky is very umber.

ALLIE
(taking in the umber sky)

Look at that. Poor LA burning again. All these fires—
All these—calamities—ahhhhh—
    Japhy, I think you knew—in my way, I did know that
I didn't do what I should have . . .

JAPHY
(nods, serious, surprised)
... Huh. Okay ... ?

ALLIE
You did love me, though.

JAPHY
Yeah ...

ALLIE
You were a true Angeleno. City of Angels. You knew
what everyone was, what I was—but I ... only you ...
knew that.

I was ...
(a whisper)
... California crazy. But I did love you too.
(beat)
Japhy ... I'm sorry.

JAPHY
Well. *Huh ...*

(a husky whisper)

"I'll be seeing you
In every lovely summer's day
In everything that's light and gay ..."

ALLIE

The Murchows, we got a nice spot here— It's— There's not a lot of stars in this section of the cemetery, but— it's a nice spot . . .

JAPHY
(singing quietly, a whisper)

". . . I'll find you in the morning sun
And when the night is new
I'll be looking at the moon—
But I'll be seeing you . . ."

Lights fade into the violent, startling red dusk of another California day.

END OF PLAY

THE
INSOLVENCIES

Note

The Insolvencies was written as a Zoom piece for a bene-fit performance of short plays for the Ojai Playwrights Conference, which was held virtually in the second summer of the pandemic, 2021. Brian Cox played Peter, and Israel López Reyes played Januz. Robert Egan directed.

JANUZ, *thirty, sitting on a stool, white shirt, blue jeans, jacket on the floor, a bottle of booze and pack of cigarettes next to him.* PETER, *sixty-five, sits in a chair, looking elegant. White shirt, gray tweed jacket. Well worn. He sips from a glass of red wine. A projection of a French cave painting from Lascaux behind them—Paleolithic paintings of bulls in earth tones fill the space—*

JANUZ

It is. It is something: I know that much, I know it is something, this thing. An isolate. Not part of any other whole. And they are little dramas; the encounters, they have acts to them. The hotel rooms.

PETER
(*a bark of a laugh*)
That one little hotel room—Jesus—with the view of the train station—

JANUZ

What happens in them—it used to be called "sex," but I think it's something else—now—and certainly with

Peter—though that certainly is part of it—I don't think he came to me for that alone. But rather for—

He closes his eyes, thinking.

PETER

The . . . act, Januz—of somehow being responsive to the close, infinite presence of another person.

JANUZ

And old men, and I mean anyone over forty-five, really—

PETER
(a bark of a laugh)

Fuck you, pal—

JANUZ
(a smile)

Old men are usually in it just for the sex, but Peter is . . . was . . . different. Particularly as everything—call it the "mood of the day," call it "the state of things"—got more frayed, more hallucinatory, more . . .

PETER

Attenuated—is the word, "attenuated." No longer just sex itself; the thing now, the thing—it's being felt. The great relief of the actual presence of an actual human who—well . . . will court the . . .

(finding the thought)
. . . the sublime dance of the "other."

JANUZ

Empathy. That's what Peter wanted, wants. In every physical part of himself.

JANUZ pours himself a Scotch and lights a smoke. PETER *nods.*

PETER

I want, or need, in this time—the age of "disconnectus extremis"—to feel the piercing sting of being seen. Simply being seen.

JANUZ

So the sex I offer is really just surrendering one's psychic armies. Much, much harder than mere sex.

PETER

Which you may know more prosaically as "intimacy."

JANUZ

Peter is more—okay, maybe much more than . . .

PETER

A tenured art history professor at the college here in town, which has only a defunct brewery, a functional typewriter company, if you can imagine, and—nestled among the old birch and oak and willows—the college.

Where Peter was—and I use this as my highest sort of compliment—in on the "joke" of everything. He knew what was—he could separate the wheat of all truths from the chaff of daily bullshit we were constantly being hosed with. He was "distinguished" . . .

PETER

It's how they would have described me once. A kind of somewhat graying, elegant, still very charming professor of "things no longer worth studying," is what they would have said once. Before it all changed, I tried to explain to undergraduates how we got from cave paintings in France to the fabrications of, say, someone like a Jeff Koons and his handmade kitsch-trash (but rendered exquisitely). My class sought to define the act of making art—from primary impulse to tell the story of a hunt to the little fucking aperçus of end-stage capitalism—all of it, our human history told through the history of its art . . .

A beat.

JANUZ
(quietly, but still amazed)
So this is it: Peter got himself into trouble over Balzac and Rodin. Yes. Honoré de Balzac by Auguste Rodin. A bronze series of Balzac himself by Rodin himself.

PETER

(laughing)

No, he's not kidding, no! You laugh? A sculpture by Rodin of Balzac—in bronze—the author with a huge belly, and then another with his dick a blurred bronze clump, a lozenge shape, casual, flaccid mostly, indifferently thick, being fondled by its owner. Balzac.

Behind them, a slide is projected, the Auguste Rodin, Balzac, Second Study for Nude F *(1896). It is projected next to the Balzac sculpture.*

JANUZ

Peter talked about it with humor and with a certain admiration for the powerful, liminal link between this penis and this creative genius—the phallus essential to Balzac's ability to write—

PETER

(laughing)

Because in order to write, Balzac would jerk off, but not cum, and drink black coffee, and write and jerk off and not cum, and repeat, a marathon fucking ritual, all fucking night and day. Rodin knew this and celebrated this complex, this compulsive, this fraught life force . . .

JANUZ
(a small smile)

And of course, because we all know how these things work now, he was then promptly invited, politely but firmly, to not ever come back to teach again.

PETER
(also entertained by this)

Because it triggered in a few of the students—these undergraduate students—an unwelcome discomfort. And claims even of "re-traumatizing" some who considered even a whiff of leering voyeurism in their professor too much to bear.

JANUZ

It was implied that Peter was being prescriptive, and that the protean energy of Balzac was somehow solely channeled through the endless fondling of his dick.

PETER

Yeah, I mean— I said to the students who gasped at Balzac's onanism shtick, "Hey, whatever works for you, right?" And I was promptly invited to the ethical committee to expand on that. Glared at by a cohort of psychosexual hysterics and harpies.

Beat. He tries to smile. Thinks.

PETER

And . . . Instead of reacting with outrage at being
fired over Rodin's rendering of Balzac's dick, I started
to shake . . . as though some trauma were being
uncovered in me. My central shame. Someone had
made sex dirty to me. Early on. You know who, of
course. Yes. Them.

Mom and Pop and church and state. Yeah. In the
part of my brain that was as old as the cave paintings
at Lascaux. Sure, sure, sure—I was sophisticated, irony
filled, and yet . . . and yet riven with an ancient sexual
shame. It had always, this shame, torn me a-fucking-
sunder.

JANUZ

I try to dislodge that shame. With my eyes, my kindness,
my mouth, my hands, my ears, the inside of me, the
outer surfaces, the secret places. I try to dislodge this
shame. To repair a good person with touch. In this time
of acute disrepair.

There is silence.

PETER
(quietly)

So, it comes about that I cook for him one night. Januz.
He sends me a note saying he missed my art history
lectures. They sent a fucking lump of clay to replace me,

a golem. So I sent him a note back. "Come over for my short ribs and a cabernet, and I will give you the rest of the semester. For free!!"

JANUZ

And I insisted on paying for his generosity with the one thing I had: my self. So cosseted and bound was Peter that it took him almost two months to finally agree.

PETER

(laughs)

One worried about the imbalance of power and shit like that, me having been his art history professor, et cetera, et cetera, et cetera . . .

JANUZ

And I had to say, "Look pal, I have the power here, you have none. What power exactly do you have over me— the history of art? Let's fuck. *Let's fuck.*" I said it again and again because I wanted it, and I wanted him to be restored. He would lie there in these beds mocking himself, and his brain and heart and body—as though apologizing for his excess twenty pounds that had in the sixty years of his life slowly managed to have cushioned him, as though being smart and witty made his need to be touched less—he would say "pathetic" and I would say "poignant."

PETER

When we finally did touch, I told him that my body, with its many secrets and scents and flaws and imperfections, had "been reactivated from a zombie slumber. From the failure of my third *long*, brief marriage . . ."

JANUZ

He called it that—"my third long, *brief* marriage." He called it that again and again, as though it had only been a season instead of eight years of an enforced, turbulent domestic cultural revolution.

PETER

It felt as though the weather never cleared and summer was always way too short within that marriage.

JANUZ *rises and slowly begins to take off his shirt.*

JANUZ

Every week there was another brilliant lecture and another fantastic dinner. There was Giacometti.

PETER

And a pork roast with morels, calvados, and pears.

JANUZ

There was Mondrian.

PETER

And a Dover sole with a buerre meunière sauce and pommes château. I mean, I could cook, mate!

JANUZ

And talk, and illuminate, and expand, and digress. Modernism! Modernism continued to light unlit places for me. And this as he . . . of course, as Peter lost his position and all the other positions he had.

PETER
(amused)
And of course, because this is how everything works now, it makes the papers: "Art History Professor Fired for Obscene Lectures."
(beat)
My book on the erotic in German Expressionism was canceled.

JANUZ

His lecture series on a Baltic cruise.

PETER

Which I had done every few summers for years, something one could never afford on an academic's pay.

JANUZ

His name on the masthead of *Apostrophe* magazine was removed.

(beat)

Then. He was accused of "grooming" students for future affairs. Even though I was his one and only one.

PETER

It became . . . "the story." One side used it to tell of cynical youth determined to burn the house down in order to reorder the privileged power structures in academia—the other to trumpet the taking down of another toxic male. The two sides fired upon one another using shrapnel made from little parts of me that they sliced off like I was a fucking shawarma slowly roasting, fat dripping off of me to sizzle into nothing.

JANUZ *takes another drink, shirtless.*

JANUZ

Peter laughed first. Thought it would pass. But then he was cracked wide open, and you could see the bewilderment in his eyes, and then he did what anyone would do, the thing they all wanted— He fucking . . . left. He left for some cave somewhere to draw in the dark, riven with his shame. I tried—and failed—to dislodge that deep, ancient, atavistic, chalky shame.

PETER

With your eyes, your kindness, your mouth, your hands, your ears, the inside of you, the outer surface of you, the secret places of you. You tried to dislodge that shame, to restore some—

He stops.

                              JANUZ

And I failed.

And PETER *quietly darkens. As though emerging out of a Goya black painting.*

                              PETER

But maybe it was too late for restoration. It was time only now for the falling, the endless falling, like a felled hunter from a cave painting, gored by . . . some new kind of heedless buffalo. I have, I will say, come to appreciate the falling. It isn't pleasant, but once pleasure and normal life, whatever the fuck that is, has been taken away from you, there are other things . . .

There's sitting in a bus while it drives through the night to some city, some little place in the mountains maybe, where there are still untested and unshorn trees. (I look at the trees and say, "Just wait, pal, they's a-coming for you too . . ."). I have dreams too. Of confronting all the committees, all the committees across the land made up of the young and the old and the young old. And the old young.

But I do think time will confront them in the form

of my favorite thing—irony—which will cause them to look at what they've done to others and wonder why this—say—glioblastoma, perhaps, has stricken them. I dream of them remembering their committees, their briefs, their secretive, anonymous pilings on and shivering slightly as their days, like mine, grow shorter . . . like mine are—shorter as the buses take me in a grid pattern through nowhere. Like a kind of muted Mondrian through nothing.

JANUZ

. . . And so now—now—I must protest on your behalf.

LIGHTS widen to reveal:

JANUZ is in the center of an art class, naked suddenly. He is a nude model. He stands there as the class of young artists try to draw him. He puts his hands on his dick, exactly like the Rodin sculpture of the naked, potent Balzac.

JANUZ

In revenge. For the things taken by the fire—justice, love—for all the attenuation. And the lost . . .

He struggles to find the words.

PETER
(quietly and clearly)
Lost act, my boy, of somehow being responsive to the

close, infinite presence of another. And that is gone. The piercing sting of being seen.

JANUZ
(to the art students, holding his dick)

Of being seen. All of you, being seen. Including this lozenge, this lump of clay.

Defiant, JANUZ *stands facing us, for all to see.*

Fade out as PETER *just looks out at us.*

END

~

Acknowledgments

I would like to acknowledge my long relationship with Center Theatre Group in Los Angeles, whose late founding artistic director, Gordon Davidson, is someone I miss greatly. He was followed by the courtly Michael Ritchie, who was my stage manager back in 1992, with *Three Hotels*. Michael went on to run Williamstown Theatre Festival and then CTG, where he never said no to me and continued to produce whatever play I nervously handed him. I would be remiss if I did not acknowledge how important the Ojai Playwrights Conference has been to me for the last two decades. Robert Egan, the artistic director for all those years, also directed these plays, and many others, starting with *The Film Society* in 1987. I sometimes find it hard to believe how far we have come together, since back then Bob had to remind me that it might be useful to have a notebook when hearing notes, a concept that had not occurred to me at age twenty-five, when we began our collaboration. I am now sixty and carry a notebook everywhere, pretty much. The actors Judith Light and Tommy Sadoski helped develop *I'll Be Seein' Ya* at various points, a reminder that playwrights need actors with an abundance of taste, boldness, bravery, wit, and a sense of humor as much as they need a notebook.

Robbie Baitz
Rancho Mirage, California
May 2022